The Knight Who Could Knit

Written by Teresa Heapy

Illustrated by Davide Ortu

Collins

Once there was a knight named Nicholas, who liked to knit. He was a very quick knitter.

He knitted scarves, hats and socks for many people.
He knitted jumpers, gloves and blankets for giants and bears.

Nicholas was good at measuring wool and tying knots.
He kept all his knitting in a knapsack.

3

Nicholas worked with lots of other knights.

Their job was to look after Queen Sharon, Princess Pam and Prince Sam.

"My knuckles are cold!" said Princess Pam.
"My knees are freezing!" said Prince Sam.
"My nose is icy!" said Queen Sharon.

Nicholas knitted gloves, socks and hats for the royal family.

The other knights made fun of Nicholas's knitting.
"Knights don't need knitting!" said a knight called Chris.
"We wear shiny metal and chain mail."

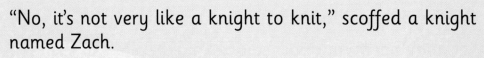

"No, it's not very like a knight to knit," scoffed a knight named Zach.

"You need to put down your needles and learn how to joust like the other knights."

Nicholas felt a bit sad, but he knew his knitting was needed.

Suddenly, there was a loud HOWL!

Nicholas, Chris and Zach looked in the air and saw a dragon heading in their direction!

She was unusually small.

"We can fight her!" yelled Zach, in a booming voice.

But the dragon ignored Zach.

She simply started gnawing at the walls.

"I will fight her!" boasted Chris, scornfully. "It will be my pleasure!"

"I'm not scared! I'll race you!" shouted Zach.

But the dragon was quite fierce.
"HELP!" yelled the knights.

The dragon chased them all to the tallest tower.
She gnawed at the walls again.

"She's wrecking the palace!" Chris yelled.

The dragon turned. She began to advance on the knights.

She got ready to pounce.

Zach winced. "We have no chance!" he said.
His knees knocked.

Nicholas knew what to do.
He knitted a very long scarf in double-quick time.

The knights dropped the scarf out of the tower.
They all climbed down it.
"Good! We're safe!" sighed the knights.
But the dragon started to cry.

"What's wrong with her?" asked Sam.

"I think she's got toothache!" said Nicholas. "Gnawing must make her feel better."

"She needs to go to the chemist for some pills!" suggested Princess Pam.

"No, I know what she needs," cried Nicholas.

Quickly, Nicholas knitted a hat and scarf.

He climbed up the tower, and he wrapped the scarf round the dragon.

The dragon nuzzled him.

I think she feels better! She will stop gnawing now.

"Well done, Nicholas," gushed Queen Sharon.

"Don't mention it," he said, bashfully.

"You are quite a character, Nicholas," commented Zach.

"You have shown you are a noble knight!" agreed Chris.

All the knights decided that knitting was excellent.
So now Nicholas runs a knitting school for knights.

A knitting knight

Review: After reading

Use your assessment from hearing the children read to choose any GPCs, words or tricky words that need additional practice.

Read 1: Decoding

- Challenge the children to find and read aloud the words with the new graphemes being taught.
  - Ask them to find the /zh/ grapheme (as in "treasure") on page 3 (*measuring*) and page 10. (*unusually*)
  - Ask them to break the words down to identify the individual phonemes.
- Challenge the children to identify two-letter graphemes for the /n/ sound on pages 12 and 13. (*gnawing, knights*)
  - Ask them to break the words down to identify all the graphemes. (*gn/aw/i/ng, kn/igh/t/s*)

Read 2: Prosody

- Choose two double page spreads and model reading with expression to the children.
- Ask the children to have a go at reading the same pages with expression.
- Model creating voices for some of the characters. Tell the children how you use clues in the text about what the character is like to create the voice. Try out different ways to say dialogue to make it seem annoyed, sarcastic, kind or triumphant!
- Encourage the children to try out voices when they read the dialogue.

Read 3: Comprehension

- Turn to pages 22 and 23. Ask the children to use the pictures to retell the story. Challenge them to remember some of the dialogue.
- For every question ask the children how they know the answer. Ask:
  - How would you describe the character of Nicholas and why? (e.g. *skilled: can knit very fast*; *clever: helped them escape from the dragon*; *kind: helps everyone with his knitting, including the dragon*)
  - How would you describe the character of Zach? (e.g. *unpleasant: he mocks Nicholas*; *cowardly: his knees knock*)
  - How do you feel about the dragon? (e.g. *I like her and feel sorry for her because she has toothache*)
- Discuss together whether it is a funny or a scary story and why.